GEORGE WASHINGTON

1

FANEUIL HALL, BOSTON

FRAUNCES TAVERN, NEW YORK

CHRISTMAS 1776

INDEPENDENCE HALL (STATE HOUSE),
PHILADELPHIA, 1774

OLD SOUTH MEETING HOUSE,
BOSTON

PULPIT

OLD SOUTH
CHURCH GATHERED 1669
FIRST HOUSE BUILT 1670
THIS HOUSE BUILT 1729
DESECRATED BY BRITISH TROOPS 1775-76

TABLET IN THE TOWER.

REVERSE OF A MASSACHUSETTS TREASURY NOTE

BOSTON MASSACRE

SONS OF THE REVOLUTION

BOSTON TEA PARTY

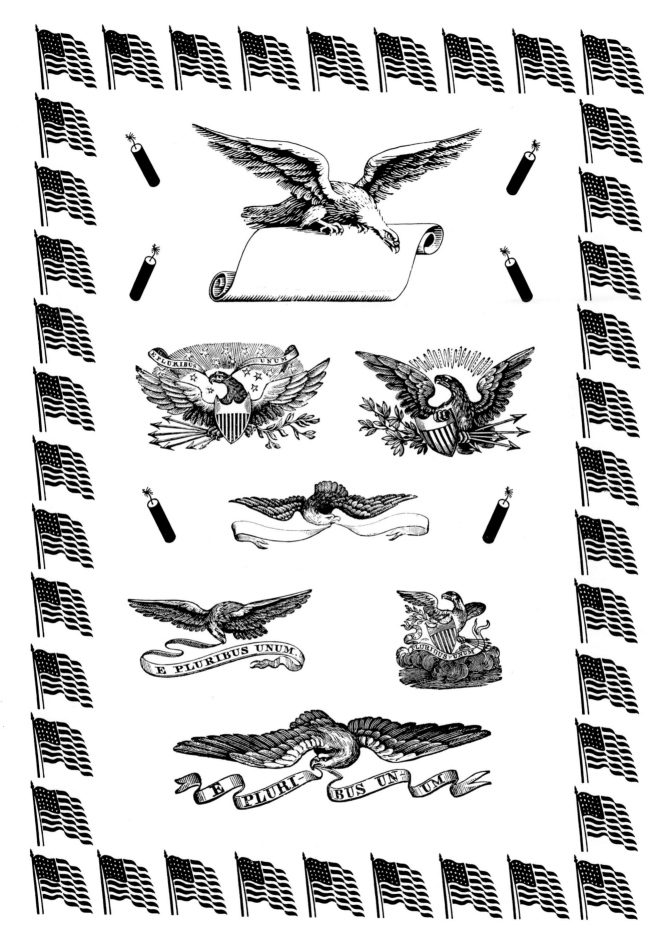

JOIN or DIE

HIS SWORD

HIS CAMP CHEST

RELIEVING GEN. CHARLES LEE

BANNER OF HIS LIFE GUARD

CROSSING THE DELAWARE

BENJAMIN FRANKLIN

BENJAMIN FRANKLIN

BENJAMIN FRANKLIN

E PLURIBUS UNUM

ALL FOR OUR COUNTRY

U.S.D. 1812.

THE GREAT SEAL OF THE UNITED STATES

ANNUIT COEPTIS

MDCCLXXVI.

NOVUS ORDO SECLORUM

LOYALTY AND PATRIOTISM
LOVE

D. OF A.

14

SIGNING THE DECLARATION OF INDEPENDENCE

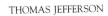

THOMAS JEFFERSON

MONTICELLO

WASHINGTON'S INAUGURATION,
FEDERAL HALL, NEW YORK

ALEXANDER HAMILTON

CELEBRATING THE ADOPTION OF
THE CONSTITUTION, NEW YORK

THE UNION STANDARD.

THE BOYS OF -61.

MILITARY ORDER OF THE
LOYAL LEGION OF THE U.S.

MADE IN U.S.A.

MADE IN U.S.A.

MADE IN U.S.A.

LIBERTY

ROBERT E. LEE

ULYSSES S. GRANT

THE SURRENDER OF LEE TO GRANT AT APPOMATTOX COURT HOUSE

ABRAHAM LINCOLN

CAVALRY

INFANTRY

E PLURIBUS UNUM

IN GOD WE TRUST.

UNITED WE STAND DIVIDED WE FALL

IN UNION THERE IS STRENGTH

THE UNION—IT MUST BE PRESERVED

DEMOCRACY

THE UNION—IT MUST BE PRESERVED

PROTECTION

ABRAHAM LINCOLN

LINCOLN IN GEN. McCLELLAND'S TENT

A CONFEDERATE FLAG

JEFFERSON DAVIS

29

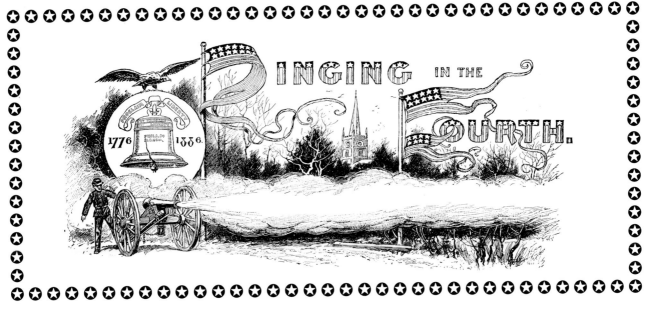

REPUBLICAN
LINCOLN
PROSPERITY

DEMOCRATIC
JEFFERSON
★ Progress ★

EMMA LAZARUS